FUN WITH SCIENCE

AIR

BRENDA WALPOLE

Contents

Use the symbols below to help you
identify the three kinds of practical
activities in this book.

EXPERIMENTS

TRICKS

THINGS TO MAKE

Illustrated by Kuo Kang Chen · Peter Bull

Warwick Press
New York/London/Toronto/Sydney
1987

Introduction

You breathe in air every day of your life and the oxygen in the air keeps you alive but most of the time you hardly notice the air all around you. One of the few times you can see air is when bubbles of air are produced underwater. But it is much easier to see the effect of air on your surroundings.

When air is heated, it becomes lighter and rises. Birds and gliders use rising currents of warm air to float in the sky. When air moves, it has enough power to push sailboats along and drive windmills. When air is squashed (compressed) into a small space it has great strength. The compressed air in a car tire supports the weight of the vehicle and compressed air also helps a helicopter to rise up into the air.

As you carry out the experiments in this book you will come to understand the different characteristics of air. This will help you to answer the questions on these two pages and explain how air influences the way in which things happen in the world around you.

This book covers six main topics:

- Air and weight
- Warm air
- Air pressure
- Moving air and compressed air
- Air and the weather
- Air and burning; life; sound

A blue line (like the one around the edge of these two pages) indicates the start of a new topic.

▲ During a storm, why do you see the lightning before you hear the thunder? (page 39)

▼ How does an airplane take off and stay up in the air? (pages 28–29)

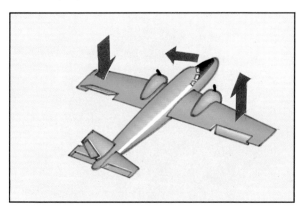

◄ Why does a parachute fall down to earth slowly? (page 26)

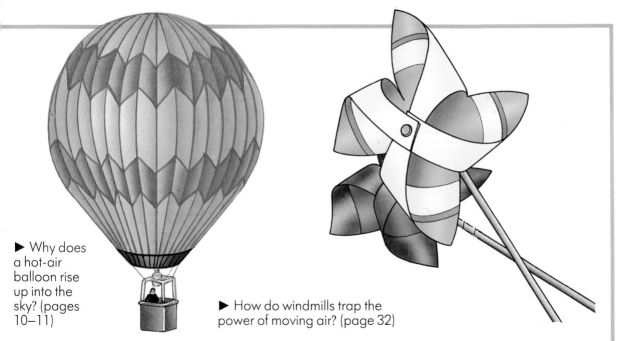

► Why does a hot-air balloon rise up into the sky? (pages 10–11)

► How do windmills trap the power of moving air? (page 32)

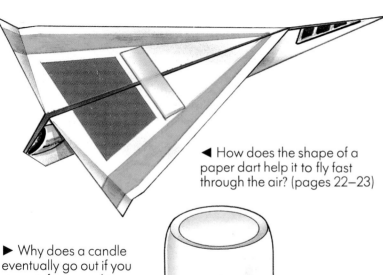

◄ How does the shape of a paper dart help it to fly fast through the air? (pages 22–23)

▲ How fast can the wind travel? What damage can a hurricane cause? (pages 30–31)

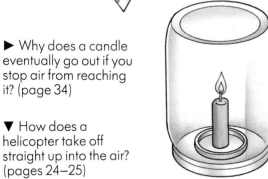

► Why does a candle eventually go out if you stop air from reaching it? (page 34)

▼ How does a helicopter take off straight up into the air? (pages 24–25)

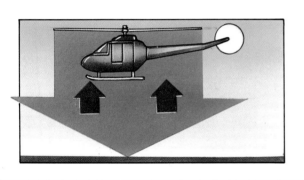

► How does double glazing help to keep a house warm? (page 13)

Where is Air?

Air is all around you but it is difficult to investigate because you cannot see, taste, or touch it. Air does not smell either, although it is possible to detect the scent of flowers, cooking, gasoline fumes, and other substances, which are carried by the air. You can feel air when it moves however, and see the effect it has on other things. It makes grass or trees sway and bend, it pushes litter along the street, and makes clouds move.

Looking for Air

As well as being all around us, air fills tiny spaces in all sorts of things. You can see this air by putting objects underwater and watching for bubbles of air to escape.

1. Push a bottle underwater and let it fill up. As water rushes in, bubbles of air rush out.

2. Now try a clay flower pot and then a small amount of soil. How much air do they contain?

3. Investigate water itself next. Place a glass of water in a warm place for about an hour. You will see small bubbles of air rising in the water or collecting on the sides of the glass. As the water gets warmer, some of the bubbles escape into the air. When water boils, a lot of large bubbles of air escape. This shows that there is air in water itself.

Divers strap tanks of air on their backs so they can breathe underwater. When they breathe out, bubbles of used air escape into the water. This is an archaeologist on an underwater dig.

Fill a Glass With Air

1. Turn one of the glasses upside down. Keep it straight and push it under the water. You will see that it stays full of air.
2. Hold the glass of air under the water with one hand and put the second glass under the water with the other hand. Turn the second glass on its side as you lower it so it fills with water.
3. Move the two glasses together and tilt the first glass so that bubbles of air begin to rise into the second glass.

How it works
Water in the second glass is driven out by air rising from the first glass. The first glass fills with water, which replaces the lost air.

Equipment: Two clear glasses, a large bowl of water.

Air Needs Space

Equipment: A clear plastic bottle, a funnel, modeling clay, knitting needle or pencil.

Seal with modeling clay.

Hole in modeling clay.

Air fills spaces that look empty. Try an experiment to test this.
1. Put the funnel in the neck of the bottle and seal up the gap using modeling clay.
2. Pour some water into the funnel. You may be surprised to see that the water does not flow into the bottle.
3. Use the knitting needle or pencil to make a small hole in the modeling clay. What happens?

How it works
The bottle was full of air but the modeling clay stopped the air escaping. When you made a hole in the clay, the air was able to get out of the bottle as water rushed in to fill the space. This can also happen in reverse. You cannot pour liquid from a can if there is only one small hole in it. As you tip the can, the liquid inside seals the hole and air cannot get inside to replace the liquid. If you make another hole in the can, air can get in as the liquid flows out.

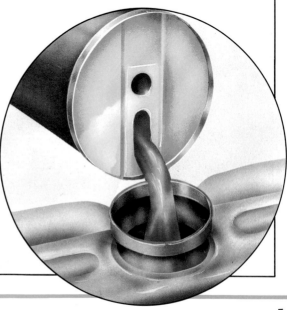

As Light as Air

Air takes up space all around us but how much does it weigh? Scientists use complex and delicate instruments to measure the weight of very light substances. You can weigh air by making a simple balance like the one in the diagram below.

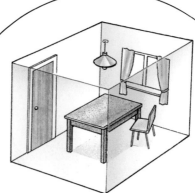

Did You Know . . . ?

The air in a large room in your house weighs about as much as a person (160 pounds or 72 kilograms).

Weighing Air

1. Mark the middle of your stick.
2. Rest the pencil between the cans and place the middle of the stick across the pencil so the stick is level.
3. Use a small piece of sticky tape to fix a balloon onto each end of the stick. Check that the stick remains level – this means that the balloons weigh the same.
4. Unstick one of the balloons and blow as much air into it as you can.
5. Fix it back onto the end of the stick and replace the stick on its center spot. Does the stick still balance?

Equipment: Two identical balloons, string, a long stick, sticky tape, two cans, a pencil with flat sides.

How it works
When you stick the full balloon back on, it makes the stick dip down. This shows it is heavier than the empty balloon and the air that you blew into the balloon does weigh something.

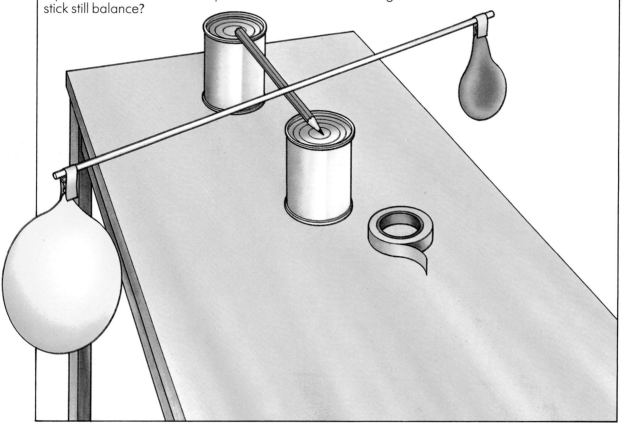

Keep the Tissue Dry

Can you put a paper tissue in water without getting it wet? All you need is a bowl of water, a small glass and a paper tissue.

Screw the paper tissue into a ball and push it into the glass. Turn the glass upside down and place it under the water in the bowl. You should find that water does not enter the glass and the tissue stays dry!

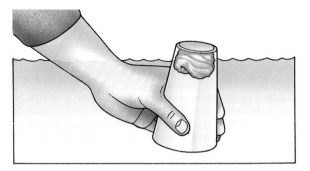

How it works
Water cannot get into the glass because it is full of air. And air cannot get out because it is lighter than water, so the tissue does not get wet.

Make a Submarine

Here is a way of making a toy submarine that goes up and down on "air power."
Equipment: A plastic bottle with a narrow neck, modeling clay, a piece of plastic tubing, coins, sticky tape.

1. Cut two or three small holes in the side of the bottle. Use the sticky tape to fix three or four coins on to the same side of the bottle. (These will act as weights and help the submarine to sink.)
2. Put the plastic tubing in the neck of the bottle and seal the neck with modeling clay.
3. Lower the submarine into the bowl of water and let it fill with water.
4. Blow through the tube to force air into the submarine. As you blow, water will be forced out of the holes in the bottom.
5. As the submarine begins to fill with air, it will slowly rise to the surface. You can make it rise and sink by changing the amount of air inside it.

How it works
Air weighs less than water. (You could test this on the balance on the previous page.) When you fill the submarine with air, it becomes lighter than the water and rises to the surface.

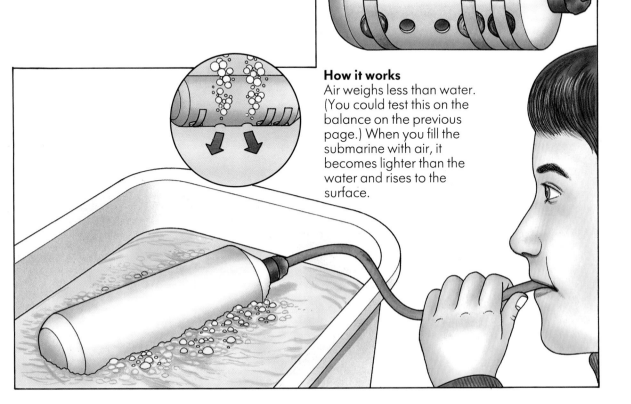

A Lot of Hot Air

Warm air is lighter than cold air so air rises as it gets warm and cold air moves in to take its place. This causes currents of air to move around inside buildings and outdoors as well. Birds float upward on rising currents of hot air and gliders stay up in the air in the same way.

Warm Air Rises

In the rooms in a house, cold air gets into the room through windows and under the doors. It is warmed by radiators, becomes lighter and rises to the ceiling. When this happens, cooler air moves in to take its place. This movement of air around a room is called a **convection current**. Warm air may escape from a room through the doors and windows again. You can find out more about how to stop the air escaping and keep rooms warm on pages 12–13.

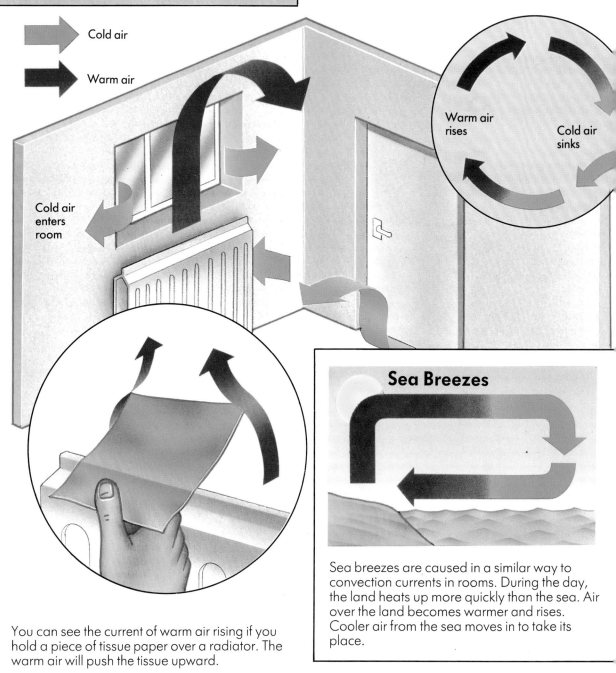

Cold air

Warm air

Cold air enters room

Warm air rises

Cold air sinks

Sea Breezes

You can see the current of warm air rising if you hold a piece of tissue paper over a radiator. The warm air will push the tissue upward.

Sea breezes are caused in a similar way to convection currents in rooms. During the day, the land heats up more quickly than the sea. Air over the land becomes warmer and rises. Cooler air from the sea moves in to take its place.

Floating on Air

Gliders have to be towed up into the sky but once they are high enough, they can use rising currents of warm air to stay up in the air. These currents of warm air are called **thermals**. At the top of one thermal the pilot has to find and reach another thermal before the glider drops too far. A glider can travel hundreds of miles on a warm day.

Make a Spinning Snake

Equipment: A square of paper, pencil, scissors, thread.

This spinning snake is a good way to observe rising air and have some fun. Draw a spiral like this on the square of paper. Decorate the snake and then carefully cut along the line of the spiral. Hang the snake above a radiator using the piece of thread and watch it spin as the warm air rises.

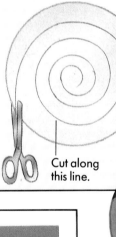

Cut along this line.

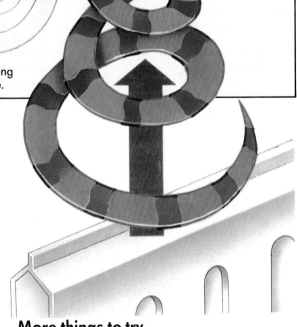

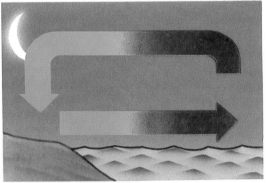

At night, the land cools down more quickly than the sea, so the sea is warmer than the land. A convection current is formed in the opposite direction to the daytime current. Warm air over the sea rises and cool air from the land moves in to take its place.

More things to try
- To keep your snake spinning longer, fix it on the tip of a pencil by making a small hole in the head end. Keep the pencil upright by placing the unsharpened end in some modeling clay or pushing it inside a cotton spool.
- Try making a "sparkling" snake using aluminum foil.

9

Investigating Hot Air

Equipment: A plastic bottle, a balloon, a deep bowl, hot water, ice.

Air takes up space but did you know that hot air takes up more space than cold air? Prove it for yourself in this experiment.

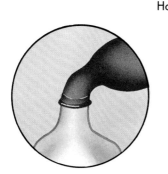

Hot water

Ice

1. Fit the balloon over the mouth of the bottle
2. Stand the bottle in the bowl and fill the bowl with hot water. After a few minutes you will see the balloon start to inflate.
3. Tip away the water and fill the bowl with ice. What happens?

How it works
When the air is warmed by the hot water, it expands and needs more space, so it stretches out the balloon. When the air is cooled by the ice, it contracts and needs less space, so the balloon goes down.

Balloon Trick

Blow up a balloon as hard as you can. Put it into a warm place, such as on top of a radiator. What do you think will happen? Warn your family that there might be a bang!

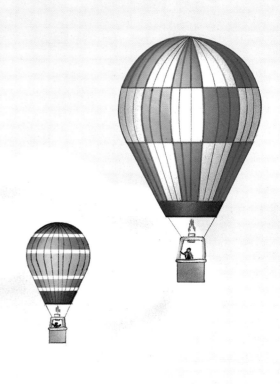

Using Hot Air

If balloons are filled with hot air, they become lighter than the air around them and float up into the air. Modern hot-air balloons have a gas burner to heat the air inside them. The wind blows the balloons along.

Today, balloons are usually filled with helium, which is lighter than air. Balloons are used for a variety of purposes, which range from advertising to carrying scientific instruments high up into the atmosphere. These instruments collect information about the weather and air pollution.

Make a Hot Air Balloon

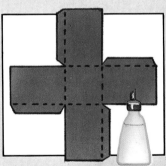

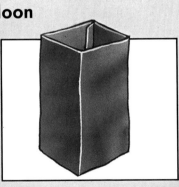

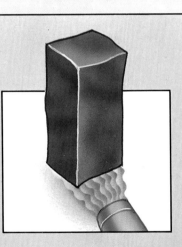

1. Glue 5 sheets of tissue paper together as shown in the diagram. (You need 1 square and 4 rectangles.)

2. Glue together the long sides of each rectangular sheet to make a balloon shape.

3. Inflate your balloon with hot air from a hair drier and it should float up to the ceiling.

Keeping Warm

Warm things cool down fast if they are left in cold air because heat travels from the warm objects into the cold air. Cold drafts make you shiver because your body loses heat to the surrounding air.

Clothes help people to keep warm. Each layer of clothing traps a layer of warm air. In very cold places, people use jackets and sleeping bags with feathers inside them. The feathers trap a lot of air and keep the people warm.

Air is trapped between layers of clothing.

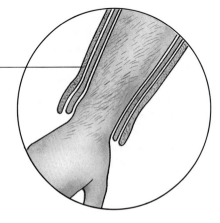

Cooling Down

Remove the lids from the four jars and wrap them up as shown in the diagrams to the right. Fill each jar with hot water and put the lid back on. Cover the lid with same wrapping as the rest of the jar. Leave the jars in a cool room for about half an hour and then take the temperature of the water with a thermometer or test the water with your little finger. Which jar contains the warmest water?

Equipment: Four jars with lids, hot water, newspaper, scarves or a blanket, thermometer, a box.

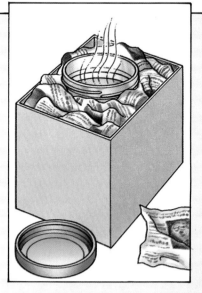

1. Put one jar in a box and wrap newspaper loosely around it.

2. Wrap a layer of newspaper around another jar. Hold the newspaper in place with elastic bands.

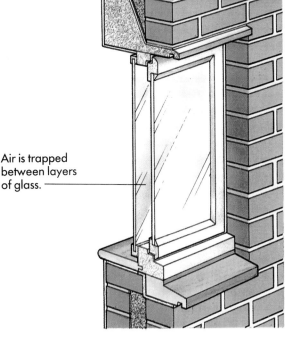

Air is trapped between layers of glass. ─────

Keeping Houses Warm

Houses also lose heat to the surrounding air when the weather is cold. Most of the heat escapes through windows, doors, and the roof. People keep their homes warm by sealing gaps around doors and windows and fitting double-glazed windows. These windows trap a layer of air between two panes of glass. This separates the warm air inside from the cold air outside and makes it more difficult for heat to escape.

3. Wrap the third jar loosely in the scarf or blanket.

4. Leave one jar without any wrapping so you can see how much effect the different wrappings have.

How it works

The warmest jar is the one that has been protected from the cool air in the most efficient way. This protection is called **insulation**. The insulation works by keeping a layer of air trapped between the warm water and the cool air outside. This helps to stop the heat escaping. The blanket or scarf and the loosely-packed newspaper both provide good insulation so the water in these jars stays warmer than the water in the other two jars.

People put insulating material in the roofs and walls of houses or wrap these materials around pipes or tanks to stop the heat escaping.

Air Pressure

When you swim underwater you can feel water pushing on your body. The air all around you does the same but your body is used to it so you do not even notice. There is more than 14 pounds of air pressing on every square inch of your skin. The pressure is caused by a layer of air called the **atmosphere**, which surrounds the earth. Most of the air is concentrated about 3 miles (5 kilometers) above the surface of the earth.

Make a Barometer

Air pressure is measured by an instrument called a **barometer**. When air pressure rises, it is usually a sign that the weather is going to improve. Air pressure falls when bad weather is approaching.

Equipment: A tall, **narrow**, clear plastic bottle, a bowl of water, paper, sticky tape, ruler, string, modeling clay.

1. Put a piece of modeling clay on one side of the bowl and use it to hold the ruler upright.
2. Fill the bowl with about 2–3 inches (5–8 cm) of water and fill the bottle three-fourths full of water.
3. Cover the opening of the bottle with the palm of your hand. Then turn the bottle carefully upside down and put the opening under the surface of the water in the dish.
4. Take your hand away from the opening but keep the bottle upright with your other hand. Tie the bottle to the ruler with the string.
5. Mark a piece of paper with a scale and stick it onto the bottle. Make a note of the water level and keep a record of how the level changes from day to day.

How it works
Air presses down on the surface of the water in the bowl. If the air pressure (the pushing power of the air) rises, more water is pushed into the bottle and the level on the scale will go up slightly. If the air pressure falls, the opposite happens.

▲ Many instruments in an airplane use changes in air pressure to give important information to the pilot. Air pressure decreases with height and this registers on an instrument called an **altimeter** (above), which shows how high the airplane is flying.

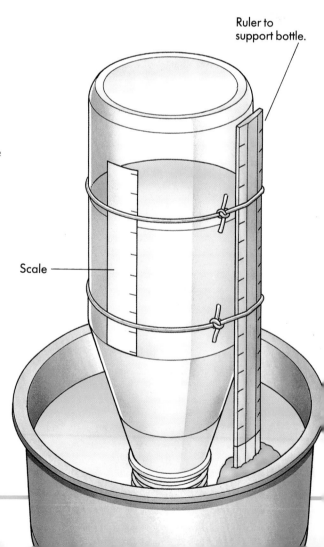

Ruler to support bottle.

Scale

The Power of Air

Air pressure is a powerful force. Here is a trick to prove it. All you need is a ruler, a large sheet of paper, and a table.

Lay the ruler on the table so about one third of it lies over the edge. Spread the paper over the ruler. Now hit the ruler and try to make the paper fly into the air. You will find that it is impossible! (Don't hit the ruler too hard or it might break.)

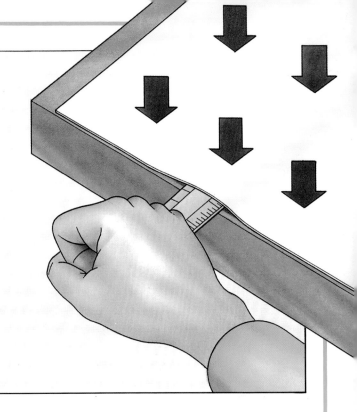

How it works
The air presses down on the sheet of paper. Because the paper has a large area, there is a lot of air pushing down on it and this is enough to stop the paper and the ruler from moving.

The Magic Glass

The pushing power of air can even keep water in a glass that is upside down! For this trick you will need a glass with a smooth rim, water and a piece of smooth card about the size of a postcard.
Fill the glass right up to the top with water and wet the rim slightly. Lay the card on top of the glass. Hold the card firmly in place and turn the glass over. Now take away your hand. The water should stay in the glass. Don't give up if it doesn't work first time – try again until you succeed.

Hint: Make sure you have a good seal between the glass and the card before you turn it upside down. It is a good idea to try this trick over a sink first!

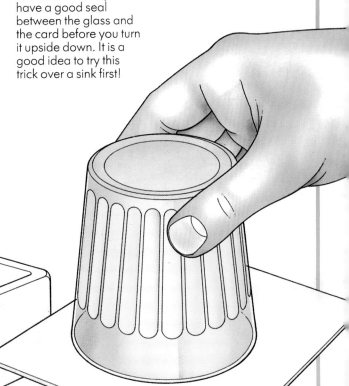

Make a Fountain

Equipment: Two glass jars (one with a lid), a bottle of water, modeling clay, four plastic straws (or a plastic tube), sticky tape, a bowl.

Seal gaps around straws.

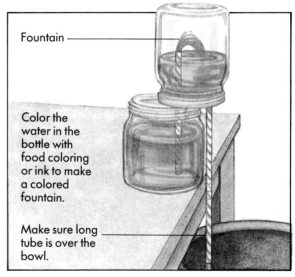

Fountain

Color the water in the bottle with food coloring or ink to make a colored fountain.

Make sure long tube is over the bowl.

1. Make two holes in the lid.
2. Push a straw through one hole so about 2 inches (5 cm) shows inside the lid. Make a long tube by fixing three straws together with sticky tape (or use plastic tubing) and push one end of the long tube through the other hole in the lid.
3. Seal the gaps between the straws (or tubing) and the lid with modeling clay.
4. Put about 2 inches (5 cm) of water into one of the jars and screw on the lid.

5. Fill the second jar three-fourths full of water and place it on the edge of a table. Position the bowl underneath. Turn the jar with the straws in the lid upside down and dip the short straw into the jar of water on the table. As you do this a fountain of water should rise up the straw.

How it works

As water from the closed jar pours down into the bowl through the longer straw (or tube), the air pressure inside the jar becomes less as the air spreads out to take up the space left by the water. The air outside is at a greater pressure than the air inside and pushes down on the water in the open jar. This forces the water up the short straw and makes the fountain.

How Straws Work

When you suck through a straw, you lower the pushing power of the air in your mouth and in the straw. The air pushing down on the surface of your drink forces liquid up the straw.

You can test this for yourself. Drink some liquid and notice how easily it comes up the straw. Then make a small hole in the straw about 2 inches (5 cm) from the top end and try to drink again. Some liquid will rise up the straw as you suck but air rushing in through the hole will try to push the liquid down again. You will be able to drink but it will take much longer and you will suck in bubbles of air too!

The Egg and Bottle Trick

Equipment: A cooked egg without the shell, a bottle with a neck slightly smaller than the egg, a piece of paper, a match or taper.

1. Check that the egg will just fit into the neck of the bottle but will not fall through. (The wide-necked bottles – carafes – that are used to serve wine are about right.)

2. Screw up the piece of paper and put it into the bottle.

3. Light the paper by using a long taper or dropping a burning match into the bottle.

4. Quickly fit the egg into the neck of the bottle. Amazingly, the egg will be sucked into the bottle with a gurgle and a pop!

How it works
As the paper burns, it uses up the oxygen in the air (see pages 36–37). The egg seals the neck of the bottle so that no more air can get in to replace the oxygen. This reduces the air pressure inside the jar and the egg is sucked in.

Air on the Move

When air moves, it has less pushing power and does not press on objects as much as still air. Objects look as if they are sucked into a stream of moving air but in fact they are pushed into the air stream by the stronger pressure of the other air around them. Objects can be pushed into the fast-moving air of a hurricane with great force.

Blow the Paper Away

Place two large books about 4 inches (10 cm) apart on a table. Lay a sheet of paper over the books. Try to get the paper to float away by blowing underneath it. Can you do it? You will find that the paper droops down in the middle as you blow.

Can you work out why this happens?

Amazing Apples

Hang up two apples about 2 inches (5 cm) apart and steady them so they hang still. Blow hard between the apples and try to separate them.

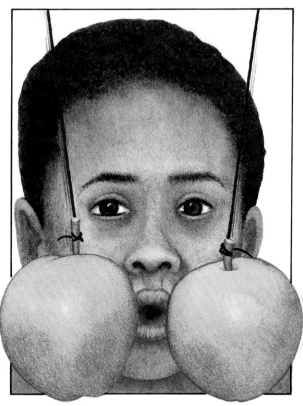

Surprisingly, the apples move toward each other! As you blow, you move the air between the apples. This moving air has less pushing power than the air on the side of the apples. So the pushing power of the air outside the apples makes them move together.

More things to try
If you are still not convinced, try the same trick using two sheets of paper. Hold them in front of your face and try to blow them apart. Once again, the moving air you blow between them should draw the sheets of paper together instead of separating them.

Make a Plant Sprayer

Use the spray to water your plants.

Equipment: 2 plastic straws, a glass of water.

1. Stand one of the straws upright in the water. It should be a little taller than the glass (trim the straw if it is too long).
2. Hold the second straw at right angles to the first one, as shown in the diagram.
3. Blow through the second straw and watch the level of water in the first straw.
If you blow gently, you will see the water rise a little. If you blow very hard, the water will rise to the top of the straw and form a spray.

How it works
The moving air blowing across the top of the straw has less pushing power than still air. The air pressing down on the water in the glass is able to push harder than the moving air and forces water up the straw.

▶ Perfume sprayers work in the same way as the plant sprayer above. The air is moved by squeezing a bulb of air.

Jumping Counter Trick

This trick shows how strong winds can lift things from the ground. All you need is a saucer and a counter.

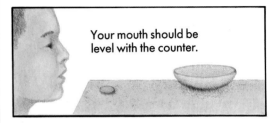

Your mouth should be level with the counter.

Place the counter about ½ inch (1 cm) from the edge of a table. Set the saucer a little way beyond it.

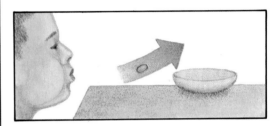

Blow strongly across the top of the counter. With some practice, you should be able to lift the counter into the saucer.

More things to try
You can make the trick more fun by drawing a target with scores and challenging your friends to a game.

Air Streams

In 1738, a Swiss scientist called Bernoulli discovered that moving air has less pushing power than still air. He did not realize that one day his idea would be used to lift airplanes.

Make a Wing

This experiment will help you to understand how an airplane wing is designed to lift such a heavy machine into the air.

Fold a small piece of paper in half and tape the top half to the bottom half about 1 inch (2.5 cm) from the edge. (This will make the top surface curved.) Slide the ruler into the fold of the wing. Then blow to direct a stream of air toward the wing. You will see the wing rise into the air as you blow.

Lift a Paper Strip

Hold a sheet of thin paper in front of your face just below your lips. Blow steadily over the top of the paper. What happens? Your breath moves the air above the paper, which reduces the pushing power of that air. The air pressure underneath the paper remains normal and this stronger air pressure lifts the paper upward.

Air flow speeds up so air pressure is low

Air flow is normal so higher air pressure pushes wing upward.

The air flowing over the curved surface on the top of the wing moves faster than the air underneath the wing. This makes the air pressure above the wing lower than the pressure underneath. The greater pressure underneath the wing pushes it up into the air. The wings on an aircraft are a similar shape to help them lift the plane off the ground (see pages 28–29).

Hovering Card Trick

Equipment: A cotton spool, a 3-inch (8-cm) square of light card, a thumb tack.

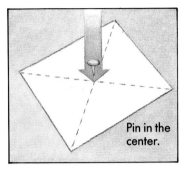

Pin in the center.

1. Join the corners of the card with diagonal lines across the square. The point where the lines cross is the center of the card.
2. Push the thumb tack through the center of the card.
3. Hold the card under the cotton spool so the thumb tack is in the hole.
4. Lift the card and the cotton spool and blow hard down the hole. Take your hand away. Can you blow the card off the reel?

How it works

The stream of air you blow down the spool passes between the spool and the card. This moving air has less pushing power than the air below the card and so the card is pushed up onto the spool.

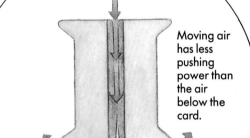

Moving air has less pushing power than the air below the card.

Air pressure pushes card upward.

Hiding from the Wind

Have you ever tried to shelter from the wind behind a tree? This experiment will show you why it does not always give you much protection.

1. Fix a candle firmly to a saucer, place it on a table and light it.
2. Place a bottle in front of the candle.
3. Blow from behind the bottle toward the candle and watch what happens to the flame.

The flame will go out because the stream of air joins up again on the other side of the bottle with the same strength as before.

More things to try

● Move the candle a short distance from the bottle. What happens now?
● Remove the bottle and blow down a funnel. Can you explain what happens to the flame?

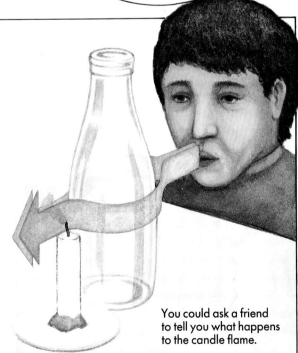

You could ask a friend to tell you what happens to the candle flame.

Fly Through the Air

Paper darts fly well. Their streamlined shape makes them shoot through the air and you can throw them accurately for a long way if they are carefully folded. Racing cars and fighter aircraft have a smooth, slim, streamlined shape to help them move rapidly. Air can flow easily over their bodywork and does not hold them back.

Making Paper Darts

All you need to investigate streamlining is two pieces of paper about 1 foot (30 cm) × 8 inches (20 cm).

Take one piece of paper and try throwing it. You will find it only travels a short distance before it floats to the ground. Next squash the same piece of paper into a ball. This time the paper should travel quite a long distance when you throw it. But its shape soon makes it sink to the ground.

Now make a paper dart by folding the other piece of paper as shown in the diagrams below.
How long will your dart stay in the air?
How far can you throw it?

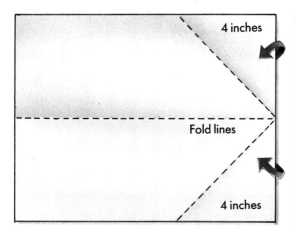

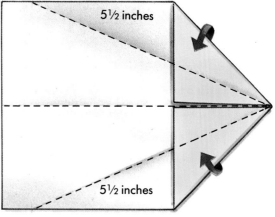

1. Measure the center of the shortest side of the paper and draw a line down the middle. Measure 4 inches (9.5 cm) down each side and draw a line to the top of the paper.

2. Fold along the lines you have just drawn. Then measure 5½ inches (14 cm) further down and draw two more lines to the center of the paper at the top.

► The streamlined shape of Concorde helps it to fly at 1,450 miles per hour (2,333 kilometers per hour) — faster than a rifle bullet. Concorde can fly across the Atlantic Ocean in just three hours.

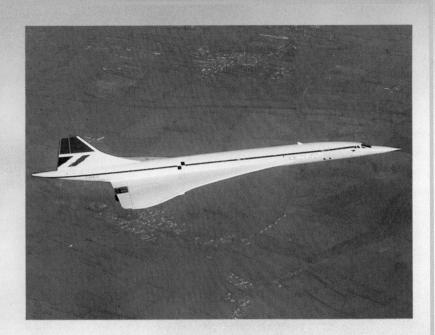

More things to try

- Curve up the top surfaces of the wings. This should help the dart to fly for longer.
- Make flaps at the back of the wings. You may have seen flaps on airplane wings. They are used to help in take-off and landing. The flaps on your dart should make it roll as it flies.
- Weight the nose of the dart with a paperclip. What difference does the extra weight make?

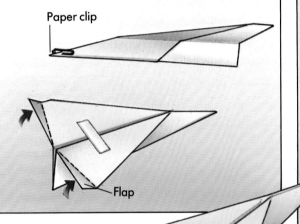

Paper clip

Flap

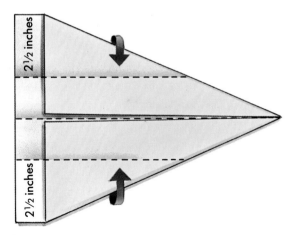

2½ inches

2½ inches

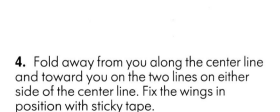

Sticky tape

3. Fold along this second line as shown. Then measure 2½ inches (6.5 cm) from each side of the bottom edge of the paper and draw a line straight up to the top.

4. Fold away from you along the center line and toward you on the two lines on either side of the center line. Fix the wings in position with sticky tape.

Squashing Air

If you pump up a tire, it begins to fill with air. As you keep pumping, you force in more and more air. Inside the tire, the air is squashed into a small space. This is called **compressed air**. It has great strength and can support bicycles and automobiles.

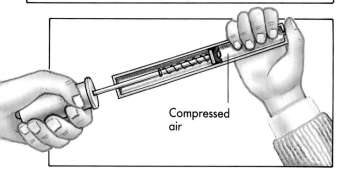

Compressed air

▲ Compressed air is strong enough to break up concrete. It is used to power drills.

◀ Hold your finger over the end of a bicycle pump as you push the handle down. As you squash the air into a smaller space, it becomes harder to push the handle down.

Lifting Books With Air

Show a pile of heavy books to your friends and ask if they can lift them using only their breath. Impossible they will say! Then show them how it can be done.

Lay a large plastic bag on a table and pile the books on top. Leave the open end of the bag sticking out. Blow into the bag keeping the opening as small as possible. Take your time and you will see the books rise off the table. They are supported by the compressed air in the bag.

Make a Helicopter

Compressed air helps a helicopter to lift off the ground. As the rotors on the top of the helicopter spin around, they push air down. This squashes the air under the rotors and the compressed air pushes the helicopter upward.

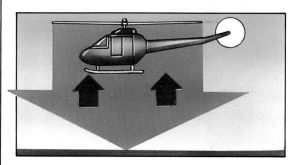

Compressed air pushes helicopter up into the air.

1. To make the rotors, trace over the cross shape on the next page.
2. Fold along the dotted lines shown. Fold one side of each rotor up and the other side down.
3. Fix the thin stick through the hole in the rotor and stick it firmly with tape or glue.

Make a Rocket

Equipment: A soft plastic bottle (a dishwashing liquid bottle will do), 2 plastic straws (one narrower than the other), modeling clay, glue.

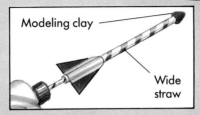

Narrow straw

Modeling clay

Wide straw

1. Make a hole in the cap of the bottle and push the smaller straw through. Seal the joint with modeling clay or glue. This makes the launch pad.

2. Then make the rocket. Cut about 4 inches (10 cm) off the larger straw. Decorate one end with paper triangles. Make a "nose" for the other end with modeling clay.

3. Slide the rocket over the launch pad. Squeeze the plastic bottle firmly and watch the compressed air in the bottle push the rocket into the air.

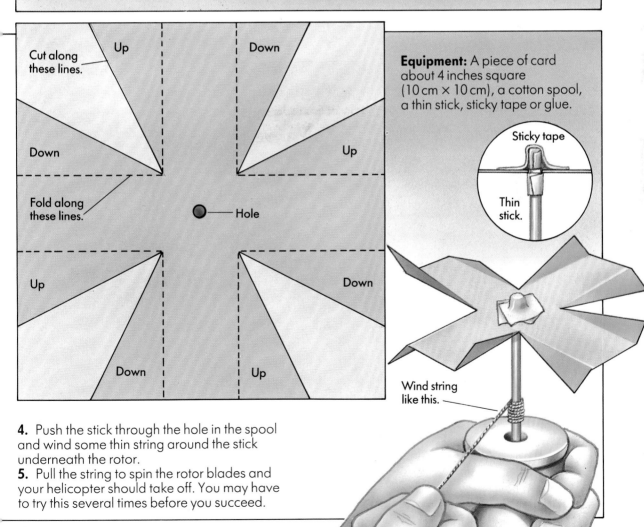

Cut along these lines.

Up

Down

Down

Up

Fold along these lines.

Hole

Up

Down

Down

Up

Equipment: A piece of card about 4 inches square (10 cm × 10 cm), a cotton spool, a thin stick, sticky tape or glue.

Sticky tape

Thin stick.

Wind string like this.

4. Push the stick through the hole in the spool and wind some thin string around the stick underneath the rotor.

5. Pull the string to spin the rotor blades and your helicopter should take off. You may have to try this several times before you succeed.

As a parachute falls, air is trapped inside the "umbrella" part. This air is squashed (compressed) so it has greater pushing power than the air around. It presses up from under the parachute and pushes it upward. The push is not strong enough to stop the parachute falling but it does slow it down. Most parachutes are umbrella-shaped but some are special shapes or have extra panels to allow parachutists to steer them.

Parachute Tests

Choose a suitable high place (such as a chair or the side of a staircase) from which to drop the toy or other object to be parachuted. First drop the object and notice how long it takes to fall. Then try dropping it attached to three different kinds of parachutes:

1. A squashed up ball made from an 8-inch (20-cm) square piece of paper.
2. A flat piece of paper the same size as the one you squashed.
3. A piece of paper 14 inches (35 cm) square. Which parachute takes the longest time to fall? (Take care to drop the parachutes from the same height each time.)

You should find the largest parachute takes the longest time to fall because it has the most air pushing up underneath it to slow it down.

Equipment: Paper, string, sticky tape, a small, unbreakable object.

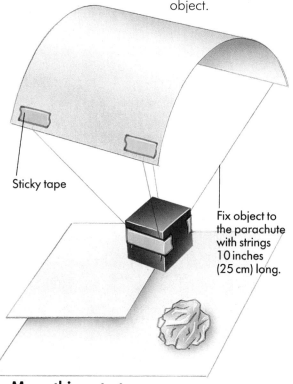

Sticky tape

Fix object to the parachute with strings 10 inches (25 cm) long.

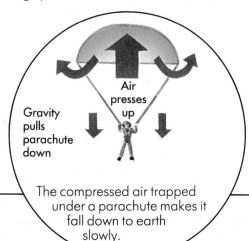

Gravity pulls parachute down

Air presses up

The compressed air trapped under a parachute makes it fall down to earth slowly.

More things to try
● Longer strings
● A hole in the top of the parachute.
● Different shapes (such as circles).
● Different materials (such as plastic or cotton).

Making a Kite

Kites work in a similar way to parachutes. As a kite is held into the wind, air is squashed under it. This compressed air pushes the kite upward so it can fly. Kites are made of very light materials so they stay up in the air easily.

Equipment: Thin material about 3 feet × 2½ feet (1 meter × 75 cms), thin sticks, a ball of string, sticky tape, glue, scissors, needle, thread.

1. First choose two sticks to make the framework. The exact measurements are not important but one stick must be twice as long as the other. Make a cross shape with the sticks and bind them together with string. Then join the corners with short sticks or string to make a diamond shape.

2. Lay the frame on top of the piece of material. Carefully cut the material around the frame leaving about 1½ inches (3 or 4 centimeters) all around. Fold over the material to cover the frame and sew or glue down the folds.

3. Make a tail for your kite using a piece of string about twice as long as the kite. Glue or tie the tail to the tip of the kite. Then attach two strings to the long stick of the frame – one above and one below the crossover point. Join the two ends together and tie them onto the end of the ball of string.

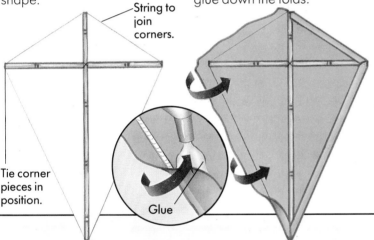

String to join corners.

Tie corner pieces in position.

Glue

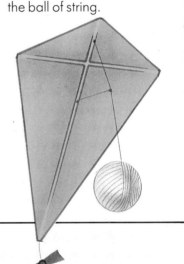

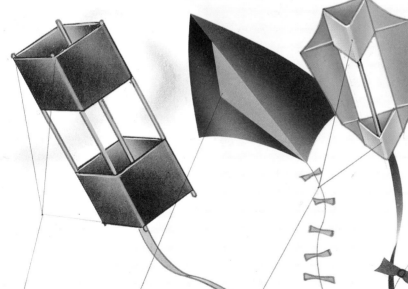

Making a kite fly

On a windy day, you can just hold your kite up into the wind. As you let go, the kite will float upward, pushed by the air. (Don't forget to unwind the string to stop the kite being pulled down again.) If it is not very windy, you can get your kite to take off by running forward into a breeze pulling the kite behind you. As you run, air is squashed into the kite and this lifts it up.

27

Looking at Flight

How do heavy airplanes get off the ground and stay up in the air? The answer is the pushing power of air. An airplane is able to lift itself off the ground partly due to its speed (which is produced by its powerful engine) and partly due to the shape of its wings.

The smooth, **streamlined** shape of the plane allows air to flow easily over its surface. This helps to reduce the drag caused by the air pushing against the plane and allows it to move rapidly through the air.

How Planes Fly

All planes need air pressure under their wings to stay up in the air. As they move forward, the higher air pressure underneath their wings pushes them upward and gives them **lift**.

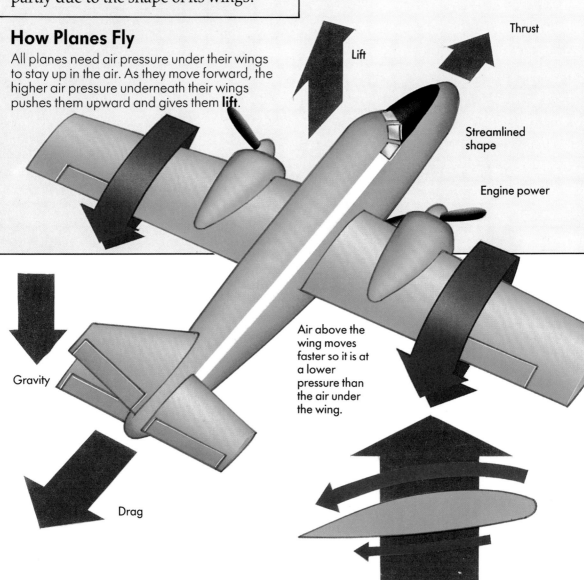

Lift

Thrust

Streamlined shape

Engine power

Gravity

Air above the wing moves faster so it is at a lower pressure than the air under the wing.

Drag

Planes move forward using engines. This movement is called **thrust**. Moving forward keeps a stream of moving air passing over the wings, which allows the plane to stay up in the air. If the engines fail, the plane will begin to descend very quickly.

Air under the wing moves more slowly and is slightly squashed so it is a at higher pressure than the air above the wing.

Diving

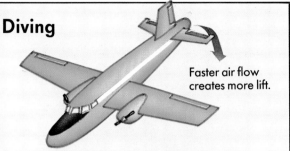

Faster air flow creates more lift.

Two small panels (called **elevators**) on the tailplane are lowered. This pushes the tail up and the nose down. To make the plane climb, the elevators are raised.

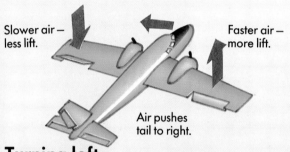

Slower air — less lift.

Faster air — more lift.

Air pushes tail to right.

Turning left

The rudder is moved to the left and a panel (called an **aileron**) on the left wing is lifted up. The aileron on the right wing is moved down.

How Birds Fly

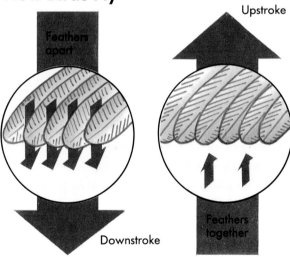

Upstroke

Feathers apart

Downstroke

Feathers together

Most birds can fly. They use their wings, feathers, and feet to do all the things a plane does with its wings and engines. During take-off, a bird pushes down with its wings and its feet to produce **"thrust"** and **"lift."** Once they are up in the air, the feathers on birds' wings can be moved to allow them to slow down, fly higher or float on the air currents. The feathers on a bird's wing are arranged so that the top surface curves upward. This helps to give extra "lift" by making the air on the upper surface of the wings move faster.

Engines

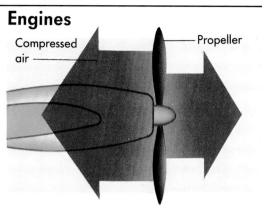

Compressed air

Propeller

Some planes have propeller engines. As the propeller blades turn, they squash (**compress**) the air behind them and the pressure of this air pushes the plane forward.

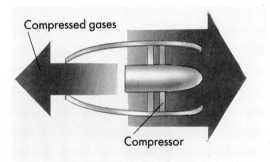

Compressed gases

Compressor

Jet engines suck in air at the front and, as their fuel burns, they shoot out very hot, compressed exhaust gases at the back. These gases are at high pressure and push the plane forward.

Wind and Weather

Changes in temperature and pressure make large sections of the air move about. This moving air is called the wind. The direction of the wind and the speed at which it moves affects our weather. Information about the wind is gathered from weather stations, ships, and satellites out in space. The data is used to predict the weather.

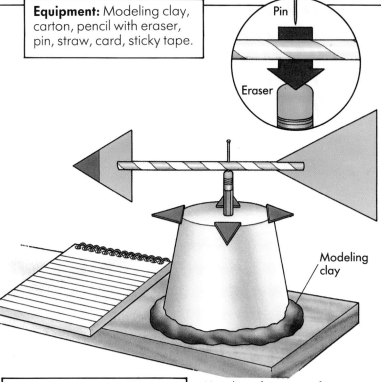

▶ Look out for unusual wind vanes. This one is on the top of a church steeple.

Make a Wind Vane

Equipment: Modeling clay, carton, pencil with eraser, pin, straw, card, sticky tape.

1. Make a hole in the middle of the bottom of the carton and push the pencil into the hole.
2. Fix the carton to the thick card with modeling clay.
3. Cut two small triangles of thin card and fix one in each end of the straw.
4. Push the pin through the middle of the straw and into the eraser.
5. Put the wind vane on a flat surface outside. Use a compass to mark north, south, east, and west on the carton. (If you do not have a compass, look at the sun. It rises in the east and sets in the west.)

Push pencil through hole in carton.

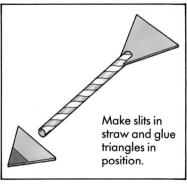

Make slits in straw and glue triangles in position.

Use the information from your wind vane to make a chart showing which direction the wind is blowing **from** each day. Weather forecasters always talk about the direction that the wind is blowing **from**. A west wind blows from the west to the east, for example. Does the direction of the wind affect the weather in your area?

How Fast Does the Wind Move?

In 1806, an English admiral called Sir Francis Beaufort worked out a scale from 0–12 to indicate the strength of the wind. His scale was based on the effect of the wind on objects such as trees and houses. The speed of the wind was added later. The scale is used today if there are no instruments available to measure wind speed.

The strongest winds on the scale are called hurricanes, typhoons or cyclones. They travel at more than 95 miles per hour (150 kilometers per hour).

Force: 0 **Strength:** Calm
Speed: Under 2½ mph
Effect: Smoke goes straight up.

Force: 1–3 **Strength:** Light breeze
Speed: 2½–15 mph
Effect: Small branches move.

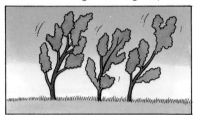

Force: 4–5 **Strength:** Moderate wind
Speed: 15–29 mph
Effect: Small trees sway a little.

Force: 6–7 **Strength:** Strong wind
Speed: 30–45 mph
Effect: Big trees sway a little.

Force: 8–9 **Strength:** Gale
Speed: 45–70 mph
Effect: Slates fall off.

Force: 10–11 **Strength:** Storm
Speed: 70–95 mph
Effect: Widespread damage.

Force: 12 **Strength:** Hurricane
Speed: Above 95 mph
Effect: Disaster.

▶ A dramatic view of a typhoon taken from a satellite out in space. Typhoons are violent hurricanes in the China seas. The name "typhoon" may either come from the Chinese words *tai fung* (which mean "wind which strikes") or from the Greek monster Typhoes, who was the father of storm winds.

Catching the Wind

People have invented different ways of catching the wind and using its power to push boats along or drive machines, such as windmills. You can find out more about the power of moving air by making your own windmills and boats.

▲ Windmills in the Netherlands.

Make a Windmill

Equipment: Thin card or stiff paper, the top of a dishwashing liquid bottle, a stick, a nail 1½ inches (38 mm) long.

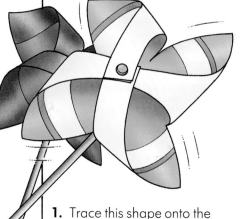

1. Trace this shape onto the thin card. Mark on the lines and dots.
2. Cut along the dotted lines and make holes through the dots.
3. Bend the four corners over and stick them together with glue.

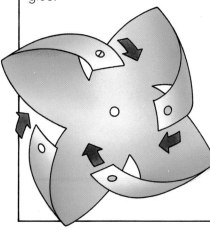

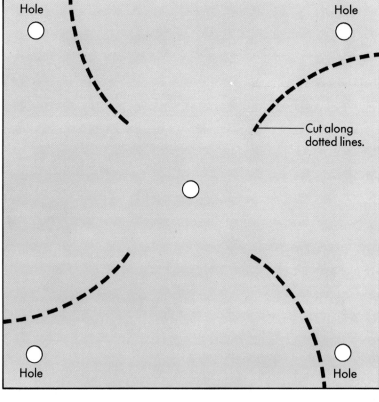

Hole

Hole

Cut along dotted lines.

Hole

Hole

Make a Sailboat

Equipment: A matchbox (or thin card), cocktail sticks or toothpicks, modeling clay, paper, scissors, bowl of water.

▼ Modern sailboats have special sails to catch the wind blowing in all directions so they can move along very rapidly.

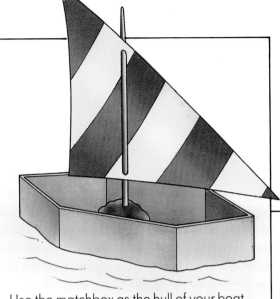

Use the matchbox as the hull of your boat (or make the hull out of thin card). Cut a sail shape from the paper and fix it to the boat using a cocktail stick or toothpick and modeling clay. Float the boat on some water and blow into the sail to make the boat move.

More things to try

Blow from different directions and see how the boat moves. Make different shaped sails for your boat. Do larger sails work better than small ones? What happens if you put two sails on your boat?

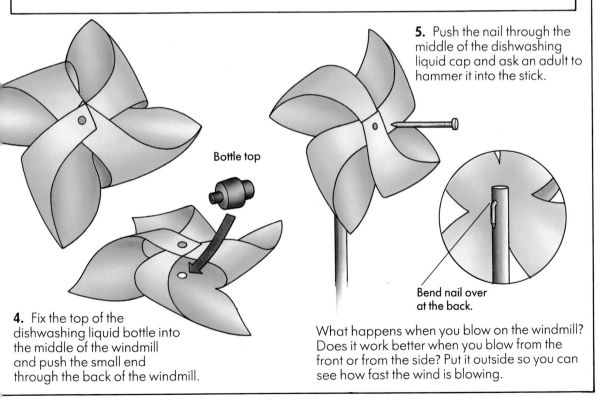

5. Push the nail through the middle of the dishwashing liquid cap and ask an adult to hammer it into the stick.

Bottle top

Bend nail over at the back.

4. Fix the top of the dishwashing liquid bottle into the middle of the windmill and push the small end through the back of the windmill.

What happens when you blow on the windmill? Does it work better when you blow from the front or from the side? Put it outside so you can see how fast the wind is blowing.

Air and Burning

Fires will not burn without air. If a fire does not burn well, people sometimes blow on it or fan the flames so that more air reaches the fire. Fires are very dangerous, so be extra careful if you do any experiments that involve fire or flames and always ask an adult to help you.

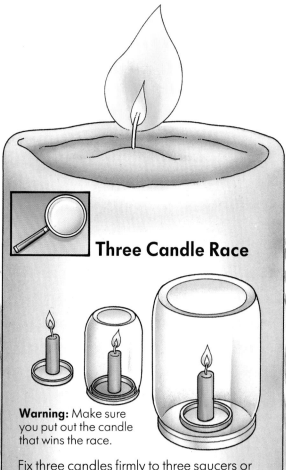

Three Candle Race

Warning: Make sure you put out the candle that wins the race.

Fix three candles firmly to three saucers or lids using modeling clay. Place them in a safe place on a table and light the candles. Leave one candle open to the air, cover one candle with a small jar and one with a large jar. Which candle burns for the longest time?

How it works
The candle with lots of air around it can keep burning after both the candles in the jars have gone out. The candle in the large jar has more air around it so it will burn for longer than the candle in the small jar.

Does All the Air Burn?

Air is used up when things burn. But only part of the air is used for burning. Try an investigation to prove this.

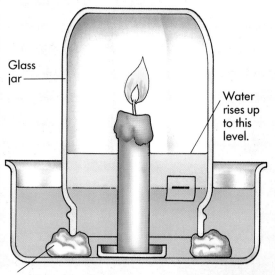

Glass jar

Water rises up to this level.

Modeling clay

Equipment: candle, modeling clay, bowl of water, large glass jar, matches.

Place the candle on its saucer or lid in a bowl of water. Make sure the candle is tall enough to be well clear of the water surface. Light the candle and cover it with the glass jar. Rest the jar on modeling clay so water can get under the rim. Mark the level of water in the jar. The candle will burn for a time but will eventually go out and you will see that the water rises up into the jar. You will find it rises about one fifth of the way up the jar.

How it works
When the candle burned, it only used part of the air in the jar. In fact it used only the gas called oxygen, which makes up about one fifth of the air. When the oxygen was used up, the flame went out and water was pushed up into the jar by the pressure of air outside. Oxygen is the part of the air that people need to live and breathe (see pages 36–37). The rest of the air is mainly a gas called nitrogen.

Make a Fire Extinguisher

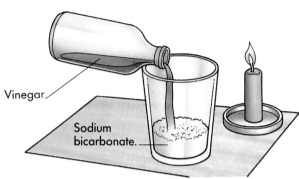

Vinegar

Sodium bicarbonate.

Equipment: A glass, a candle, a saucer, matches, a teaspoon, vinegar, sodium bicarbonate, a cardboard tube.

Carbon dioxide rolls down tube onto candle.

1. Fix the candle to the saucer or lid and place it on a table. Light the candle.

2. Put one teaspoonful of sodium bicarbonate into the glass. Pour in about 1 inch (3 cm) of vinegar. You will see bubbles appear in the glass. These are a gas called carbon dioxide, which is formed as the vinegar and sodium bicarbonate mix together.

▼ Foams from fire extinguishers keep oxygen away from the flames by covering them in a blanket of bubbles of carbon dioxide gas. Carbon dioxide does not burn.

3. To put out the candle, carefully tip the carbon dioxide gas down the cardboard tube. You will not be able to see the gas but just imagine you are pouring water down the tube. Keep the end of the tube out of the candle flame.

4. As the carbon dioxide covers the flame it will soon go out.

How it works

Carbon dioxide is heavier than air, which is why you are able to pour it down the tube. It pushes the oxygen away from the candle flame and stops it burning.

Air for Life

All living things need the oxygen in the air to survive. If people travel to places where there is not enough air (such as the tops of mountains) or no air at all (such as out in space) they have to take a supply of air with them. People also have to take air underwater with them.

The Air You Breathe

People get the oxygen they need by breathing. As you breathe in, you take air into the lungs in your chest. Inside the lungs, oxygen passes into the blood and is carried all around the body. It is used in the chemical reactions that release energy from food. The waste gas (carbon dioxide) produced in this reaction leaves your body as you breathe out. Count how many times you breathe every minute. How does this change after exercise, such as running or cycling?

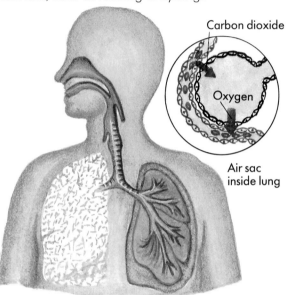

Carbon dioxide

Oxygen

Air sac
inside lung

◀ There is no air in space so astronauts have to take it with them. If they leave the spacecraft, they breathe air from special cylinders on their backs.

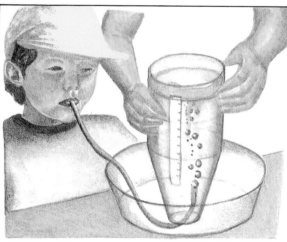

Equipment: A large plastic bottle that holds 7 or 9 pints (4 or 5 liters) of water (such as a camping container), plastic tubing 2 feet (60 cm) long, ruler, rubber bands, bowl.

How Much Air Do Your Lungs Hold?

1. Put the bowl in the sink or the bath and fill it about one third full of water. Fill the bottle to the top with water.
2. Place the palm of your hand over the top of the bottle (or put the stopper on). Quickly turn the bottle upside down and put the top under the surface of the water in the bowl. Ask someone to hold the bottle steady and take your hand away (or remove the stopper).
3. Fix a ruler to the side of the bottle with rubber bands or mark a scale on some paper and stick it onto the bottle.
4. Put the tube in the neck of the bottle. Take a deep breath, hold your nose and blow hard down the tube. How much water can you blow out in one go? This will give you some idea how much air is in your lungs.

Where Does Oxygen Come From?

Green plants are very important for life on earth because they produce oxygen. (This is why it is important for us to take care of our environment and not to cut down large areas of forest.) Green plants produce oxygen during the process they use to make their own food from carbon dioxide (another gas in the air) and water. Energy from the sun is used to power this process, which is called **photosynthesis** – this means "making things with light."

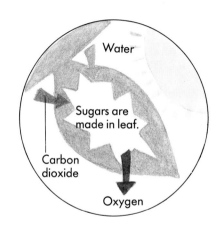

Photosynthesis takes place mainly in the leaves of green plants. Try this experiment to prove that oxygen is released. All you need is a bowl of water, a glass jar, and some water plants such as pondweed. Place the plants in the bowl of water. Fill the glass jar with water by lowering it into the bowl on its side. Turn it upside down to cover the plants. Leave the experiment in a sunny place and look at it from time to time.

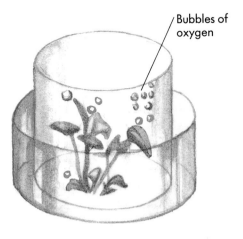

How it works
You will notice streams of oxygen bubbles rising to the surface of the water. Eventually a little pocket of oxygen will collect at the top of the jar. Water plants release oxygen into the water just as land plants release oxygen into the air.

How Polluted is the Air?

Car exhausts, factories, and power stations produce smoke, gases, and dust, which make the air dirty and polluted. Tiny plants called **lichens** can show you how polluted the air is. Some types of lichen grow where the air is polluted; others can only survive in clean air. The air is cleanest where there are a lot of different types of lichen. Look for lichens on trees and walls.

Polluted air   Clean air →

No lichens
An alga called *Pleurococcus* forms a powdery green film on trees and walls. This is a sign the air is polluted.

Crusty, gray, or green lichens
These lichens grow in town centers and can survive where the air is dirty.

Flat, rounded lichens
These may be green, yellow, black, or orange and can survive some pollution.

Bushy lichens
Usually green or gray. These are very sensitive to air pollution and will grow only where the air is clean.

Air and Sound

Air does not only carry aircraft and birds, it also carries sounds. You may be surprised to learn that there is no sound out in space, where there is no air.

Sounds travel through air rather like ripples travel across a pond. If you throw a stone into a calm pond, the water near the stone moves up and down and ripples travel outward. If the ripples bump against a small object, such as a stick floating on the water, they will make the object move up and down as well. In a similar way, sounds make the air close to them move up and down in waves. This is called **vibration**. If the vibration of the air reaches your ears, it makes the ear drum inside each ear vibrate so you can hear the sounds.

Make a Harp

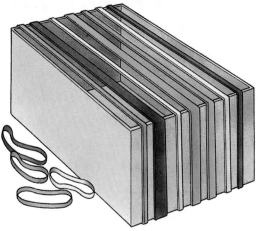

All you need is a cardboard or plastic box and eight, thick rubber bands. Stretch the rubber bands around the box and pull the bands with your fingers to play your "harp." Then put your fingers on the end of a band to stretch it tighter. The tighter the elastic band, the higher the note it makes.

Sound Waves

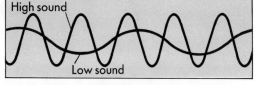

High sounds make waves that are close together. Low sounds make waves that are further apart. Just as with ripples on a pond, sound waves become weaker further away from a sound. This is why you can hear more easily when you are close to the source of a sound.

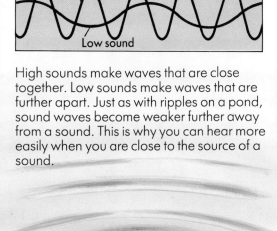

Making Music

Musical instruments make sounds in a number of different ways. Each one starts the air vibrating in its own way.

Vibrations from a drum begin when the skin stretched across the surface of the drum is hit with a special stick. The skin moves up and down and starts the flow of sound waves. Instruments with strings, such as guitars or violins, are plucked with a bow or fingers to start a stream of vibrations. Woodwind instruments have a mouthpiece. The player either blows down into the instrument to make a reed vibrate (as with an oboe or clarinet) or blows across a hole to make a column of air inside the instrument vibrate (as with a flute).

Fix a cork to a knitting needle and push it inside a cardboard tube. Blow across the top of the tube and move the needle up and down. What happens? This is how the sound is produced in a flute.

Singing Bottles

Arrange several bottles in a row. Leave the first one empty and put a small amount of water in the next one along. Put a little more water in the third bottle, even more in the fourth one and so on until you get to the end of the row. Fill the last bottle almost to the top. Tap the bottles with the spoon or blow across the top. As you tap on the glass or blow across the top of the bottle, you make the air inside vibrate. There is a different amount of air in each bottle so each one makes a different sound.

How Far Away is the Storm?

During a storm, have you ever noticed that you always see lightning before you hear thunder? When lightning flashes, it suddenly releases a great amount of heat. This warms the air, which expands with a small explosion that we call thunder. We see the lightning almost immediately because light travels fast. But the sound waves from the thunder take longer to reach our ears.

When you see lightning, count the number of seconds before you hear the thunder. Divide the number of seconds by five and this will tell you approximately how far away the storm is in miles.

Index

Editor: Barbara Taylor
Designer: Ben White
Illustrators: Kuo Kang Chen · Peter Bull
Consultant: Terry Cash

Additional Illustrations: Andrew Macdonald; pages 16–21, 24 (bottom left) Catherine Constable; pages 36, 37 Mike Saunders (*Jillian Burgess*); pages 4, 5
Cover Design: The Pinpoint Design Company
Picture Research: Jackie Cookson

Photograph Acknowledgements: 4 left ZEFA; 9 top Warren Jepson Ltd; 12–13 ZEFA; 14 top right Smiths Industries; 19 bottom Parfums Lagerfeld Ltd; 23 top British Aerospace, Civil Aircraft Div; 24 top ZEFA; 29 Roger Tidman/Nature Photographers; 30 top right J.Allan Cash; 31 bottom, 32 ZEFA; 36 left Photri/ZEFA; 39 ZEFA.

Published 1987 by Warwick Press, 387 Park Avenue South, New York, New York 10016.

First published in Great Britain by Kingfisher Books Limited.

Copyright © 1987 by Grisewood & Dempsey Ltd.

Printed by South China Printing Company. H.K. 6 5 4 3 2 1
All rights reserved

Library of Congress Catalog Card No. 86-51554
ISBN 0-531-19024-2